Spirituality of the Priesthood

by Pope John Paul II
Compiled by Leonardo Sapienza
Preface by Cardinal Angelo Comastri

*All booklets are published thanks to the
generous support of the members of the
Catholic Truth Society*

CATHOLIC TRUTH SOCIETY
PUBLISHERS TO THE HOLY SEE

Contents

Preface

A light shines before us, it is the light of Mary's "yes", a "yes" that attracts us and gently rebukes us for our "no's", a "yes" that encourages us and points us squarely in the direction of the source of joy that we all seek.

It must be clearly stated that there is a predominant "yes" in every person, there is a love of something that everything else revolves around and points to, for some this can be success, for others power, or money and for others again, an egotism that has become the purpose and idol of their whole life. We will not be resigned to placating this hunger for happiness by artificial means. Therefore we must ask which "yes" will satisfy us? Which "yes" will fulfill us and answer the deep longing of the human heart?

Mary answers this question without a moment's hesitation, "I said yes to the Lord and found the melody that made my whole life sing." St Augustine, that fervent searcher for happiness adds: "It is true! God made us for eternity and our hearts are restless until they rest in Him." That meticulous and decisive woman, St Teresa of Avila comments: "Let nothing disturb you, let nothing frighten you, everything passes and God alone remains. And God alone is enough." The young Parisian Charles de Foucauld, who searched desperately for light, when the mystery of God was revealed to him exclaimed: "As soon as I believed that God existed, I understood that I could do naught else except live for him alone. There is too big a difference between God and everything else that is not him." And many others could tell of having had the same experience.

At this point then we are faced with the irrepressible question, where can we meet God?" How can we say "yes" to him? We Christians exist to guard and spread to all, the good news that God came into our midst, he came to us and we can meet him in Jesus Christ. Jesus is the good shepherd that seeks for us, gathers us and guides us on the journey from selfishness to love, from darkness to light, from death to life, from a heart of stone to a heart that beats with the same rhythm as the heart of God.

What a task! It is the greatest task, one worthy of God, one so large that only he could take it on.

Yet - and here is the truly astonishing point - Jesus does not wish to act alone, he wants someone to make his face, his voice, his hands, his tireless feet and his heart that burns with visible love. So Jesus called some men, so that they might become shepherds with him, shepherds for him and shepherds in him. Simon he called while he was still on the lake and remembering his profession, Jesus said to him, "From now on you will be a fisher of men. To Matthew, who was protecting the money on his counting table, Jesus ordered, "Come and follow me." James and John, who under the happy eye of their old father were mending their nets, saw a new horizon being opened before them when Jesus said, "Follow me!" It's the story of the first priests and of every priest: within the Church there is the echo of this young and lovely voice calling.

How can his voice be heard? On what frequency can we listen to him? Jesus himself reveals this secret when he says, "I am the Good Shepherd and I lay down my life for my sheep!" Meaning, "My strength is love, my language is the gift of self, and whoever loves will hear! Whoever is freed from selfishness immediately perceives my voice."

Many people can testify to the truth of all this! Many young people could tell you, giving you dates and times, when the spark of their vocation ignited, thanks to an experience of service as a gift, of spending themselves for others!

And many young people have been captivated by those who have generously given themselves over to Jesus.

These are the marvellous stories and histories of priests, through whom Jesus has continued his tireless work as sower of joy, of hope and of forgiveness.

This collection gathers together enlightening thoughts on the priesthood, which came from the heart and mind of the Servant of God John Paul II. They are living, fresh and relevant reflections. In the Year for Priests proclaimed and wanted by Pope Benedict XVI, Father Leonardo Sapienza has given us this gift and we are all grateful to him.

Angelo Card. Comastri
Archpriest of the Papal Basilica of Saint Peter in the Vatican.

Introduction

In October 1990 the eighth general Assembly of the Synod of Bishops was arranged, to study the subject of "The formation of priests in our time."

Pope John Paul II gladly understood and took the opportunity, using the catecheses of the Sunday Angelus (from December 1989 to September 1990) to invite the Christian community to reflect on a subject of vital importance for the life of the Church.

He focused on the ministry of the priesthood within the Church, on what it was and what it entailed, according to the intentions of Jesus, who instituted it and remains its perfect incarnation.

In this way John Paul II illustrated the richness of the mystery that the priesthood expresses, and he highlighted the qualities that a priest needs to fulfil that mission.

It seemed useful then, in this Year for Priests announced by Pope Benedict XVI, to present once again these reflections, to help priests and lay people to better understand the figure of the priest.

The mission of the priest is one of great value, one that is difficult but fruitful, arduous but providential.

May the Lord of the harvest allow the celebration of the Year for Priests to contribute to a new springtime for the priestly vocation, that is so necessary to the life and mission of the Church.

Leonard Sapienza

Our Vocation is a Gift

The Synod of 1971 had dealt with the problems of the priestly ministry. With reference to the Gospel and in accordance with the teachings of the Second Vatican Council, the Synod fathers reiterated certain essential doctrinal principals and indicated various methods of working in regards to the ministry and life of priests. Even today, the norms they put forward retain their capacity to enlighten us.

The many difficulties which the priestly life is encountering in our day, make more obvious the urgency of an appropriate formation which fully responds to the demands of the contemporary world. It was therefore opportune that the topic of the ministerial priesthood should be completed with a deepened reflection on priestly formation. We know that the priestly vocation is a gift of grace, a gratuitous call, which proceeds from divine love; in fact, one can never consider the priestly life as a merely human promotion, nor the minister's mission as a simple personal project. In every moment of his life the priest must consider himself as the recipient of a special call from Jesus, and be totally committed to fulfilling it. Precisely in order to be fully accepted and produce all its fruits, this call requires a formation which allows the development of all that is sown by grace.

This development is not possible without a serious doctrinal and spiritual formation, to help each one called to live his priestly consecration adequately. This formation is the concern of bishops and all those who cooperate in the maturation of vocations and their successful outcome. However, all the faithful are also involved in this formation; everyone is called to share the concern of the pastoral authorities and to pray for the formation of priests. Let us ask Mary that each of us may hear the announcement with the interior disposition with which she heard the first announcement of the Good News.[1]

Christ, the Ideal Priest

Christ is the unique and eternal priest, meaning that within the Church priests are such insofar as they participate in his priesthood through their "indelible character" a spiritual sign that they have become like him, Christ. These exercise their ministry always and only in the name of, and by the authority of Christ. This is why it can be said that above all, the priest is another Christ. "Sacerdos Alter Cristus".

According to the words of the angel at the time of the Annunciation, the work of the Holy Spirit will make the child holy, or consecrated, from his birth. The Holy Spirit realises in Jesus Christ - the Messiah, the Anointed, the consecrated one *par excellence* - the first priestly consecration, source of all the others. It will always be he, in every priestly ordination, who will effect that consecration which involves the human person in the depth of his being, in order to conform him to Christ and commit him to the service of his Kingdom.

The fundamental importance of the Holy Spirit's action must not let us forget the value of Mary's cooperation. This was particularly exercised in the hidden years at Nazareth, with the education given to Jesus. Mary contributed to preparing her Son for his priestly mission, helping the development of all his human qualities. Later when Jesus will reveal his meek and humble heart, open to all with welcome and good will, full of compassion for the suffering, he will offer to everyone the fruits of a development in which Mary had a noteworthy though hidden role.

In the light of these facts one can understand that priestly formation is first of all the work of the Holy Spirit who exercises his power of sanctification, by preparing the future priest to be a man of God in the image of Christ. Such a formation awaits from Mary a help towards the development of all the human qualities which express in practice charity in social relationships, making the priest capable of entering into the situation in which he is placed.

Let us turn towards Christ who is coming, that he aids us to see ever more clearly the priest in him, from which flows every priesthood and let us ask that his model may be reflected and renewed in all those who today prepare for the priesthood.[2]

Promoter of the Faith

If our faith seems to be weak or waning we can always take refuge in Mary who - even before the birth of Jesus - was proclaimed to be blessed because she believed. It was in fact in her faith that the waiting of the people of Israel reached both its height and its fulfilment.

The fundamental importance of faith is particularly evident in the formation of future priests. If indeed this virtue is necessary for everyone, it is especially so for the priest, who has the mission of proclaiming the Word. He cannot preach the Gospel effectively if he has not deeply assimilated its message. The priest is called to bear witness to the faith by his activity and his whole life. When he celebrates the Eucharist and administers the sacraments, he shows his faith. In his pastoral contacts he must sustain his brothers and sisters in faith, answer their doubts and objections, and strengthen those who are troubled or hesitant.

When people go to the priest to ask his advice or confide to him their difficulties, they do not expect a simple, common-sense answer, but a word of faith. They are disappointed when they do not find in him an attitude of faith; on the contrary, when they recognise in him a witness of faith, they are strengthened in their convictions.

Every priest must inspire faith in the Christian community. This is a very noble mission and a great responsibility for which he must carefully prepare himself. It is therefore necessary that revealed doctrine be taught in seminaries in such a way that the young men will better understand what constitutes the object of their faith.

It is also necessary that, in preparing for the priestly ministry, education in the faith is provided for. The young people who are destined to announce the Gospel must be committed to developing their vocation in a climate of faith. Hence the need that courses of study should not only be inspired by the faith, but should also lead to an ever more solid faith, better founded upon revelation.

Let us have recourse to the Virgin of the Annunciation who responded with faith to the divine call, that she may strengthen in this virtue all those who are in charge of priestly formation.[3]

Man of Hope

Christ wants us to participate actively in the work he began by coming into the world, he desires our collaboration in his work of redemption.

The person who believes expects everything from Christ, and yet works as if everything depended on himself or herself. This is the hope which must motivate the Christian in his or her daily efforts to conform to Gospel values.

This is particularly the hope which must support the ministry of the priest, who speaks and acts in Christ's name. The priest is the man of hope.

To form a priest means to form a man who has the task of bearing witness to Christian hope and strengthening it in others.

The world thirsts for hope. It feels oppressed by many ills, afflicted by many trials. The drama of misery and the tragedies caused by human passions are found everywhere. Rivalries, wars and conflicts of every type are obstacles to our desire for peace. Requests for a just distribution of wealth meet the resistance of arrogance and selfishness. The priest, the man of hope, will encourage all the forces of good will, but will lend most of all to develop around him the "hope that does not deceive" (*Rm* 5:5), that is, the hope that turns to Christ and expects everything from him.

The priest can do this if he is formed in faith in Jesus, humanity's one and only Saviour: if he is accustomed to look at the world with the optimism deriving from Christ's victory over the forces of evil. The optimism of hope is not naive, it does not overlook the adversities which affect people and the difficulties they encounter in building a better society. However, it is based on Christ's sovereign power, which is greater than all evil and difficulties.

We express the wish that the Synod may promote the formation of priests in hope, the virtue which we ourselves try to advance in, in imitation of the Virgin Mary, whose hope was wonderfully fulfilled.[4]

The Family for Vocations

From the biblical account of creation, we know that the family was something desired by God, when he created man and woman, and blessing them said: "Be fruitful, multiply." (Gn 1:28)

The grace of Christ then, transmitted through the Sacrament of Matrimony, makes families capable of realising the union to which they are called. In particular, Christian families are pledged to reproduce the ideal expressed by Jesus in his priestly prayer, "As you Father, are in me and I in you, may they also be one in us." (*Jn* 17:21) He who made this prayer obtained a special gift of unity for all families through his sacrifice.

The Son of God became a priest in the Incarnation, but precisely in virtue of such a ministry he needed a family upbringing. Jesus obeyed Mary and Joseph, "He was subject to them" as the gospel says (*Lk* 2:51). This submission contributed to the child Jesus' union with his parents and to the atmosphere of perfect understanding which prevailed in the home at Nazareth.

The upbringing he received in the family actually prepared Jesus for the mission which he had to fulfil upon earth, according to the revelation of the angel at the time of the Annunciation. It was therefore a formation for the fulfilment of his priestly ministry, more particularly for the offering of the sacrifice of himself to the father.

Thus the role of the Christian family in the development of priestly vocations is illuminated. A vocation is a call which comes from God's sovereign power and free gift. However, such a call must find an open path in the heart, it must enter into the depth of the subject's thought, feeling and will, in order to influence his moral behaviour. The young person needs such a family atmosphere which helps him to be aware of the call and to all its virtuality.

Praying today for all families of the world, we should particularly ask Mary, Mother of God and our mother, to favour the development of priestly vocations and to bless those families which show their readiness in giving their children to the Church.[5]

The Priest in the Third Millennium

The believer asks questions about the future of the Church and therefore on the ministry of the priest in their own age. It is clearly necessary to prepare the young men called to the priesthood, so that they are spiritually equipped to enter their new period of history, and do their task of bringing the light and life of Christ to their contemporaries.

It is true that the future is unknown to us, and that no one can foresee precisely the development of human history, nor the conditions towards which the life of the peoples will evolve. Indeed we know that the future is in the hands of the Almighty, who acts upon human events from perspectives very different from ours.

Nevertheless, there is an essential aspect of the priest that does not change; the priest of tomorrow, no less than the one of today, must resemble Christ. When Jesus lived on this earth, he manifested in himself the definitive role of the priest, by establishing a ministerial priesthood with which the apostles were the first to be invested; this is destined to last in endless succession throughout the whole of history. In this sense the priest of the third millennium will continue the work of the priests who, in the preceding millennia, have animated the life of the Church. In the third millennium the priestly vocation will continue to be the call to live the unique and permanent priesthood of Christ.

Nevertheless the priesthood must also adapt itself to every era and environment of life. For this adaptation it is necessary to depend most of all on the action or the Holy Spirit who discerns the future and guides the entire Church towards new developments.

For our part we must therefore seek to be as open as possible to the higher enlightenment of the Holy Spirit, in order to discover the tendencies of contemporary society, recognise the deepest spiritual needs, determine the most important concrete tasks, the pastoral methods to adopt and thus respond adequately to human expectations.

Let us pray to the Virgin Mary that the priests of the third millennium may inspire the world with the spirit of the Gospel.[6]

Praying for Vocations

How and to what extent is it possible to help the birth and growth of vocations? It is a question that Christian parents and educators are often asked, and one that deserves to be carefully studied.

Looking at this it is important above all to remember that a vocation is rooted in God's sovereign initiative. God's decision must be respected, no one can force it or substitute a human decision for it. Only those whom Christ calls are fit for the priesthood!

This is reason why one of the principle means of promoting vocations is prayers. By praying we can see to it that callings are multiplied, "Pray of the Lord of the harvest to send workers to the harvest!" (*Mt* 9:38). A prayer like that, commanded by Christ, cannot go unanswered.

Besides prayer, other human initiatives can be useful for the blossoming of vocations. An episode in the gospel gives us an efficacious example. Andrew, one of the first two disciples who began to follow Jesus, told his brother Simon what had happened to him, and "He led him to Jesus" (*Jn* 1:42). Certainly it was Jesus who called Simon and gave him the name Peter, but it was Andrew's initiative which brought about the meeting, during which Jesus directed his call to the future Head of the Church.

The conclusion is that each of us can become an instrument of grace in the matter of vocations. There are times when something said to a young man or a simple question asked, can awaken in him the thought of a vocation. Teachers especially have the opportunity to communicate the value of priestly life. That, however must always come about with respect for the personal freedom of the young man, and in a context of sensitivity which avoids anything that could be construed as mortal pressure.

By praying for priestly vocations, we will pray also that the Synod encourage all Christians to promote them, according to the means they have at hand. May the Virgin Mary, who is full of concern for the growth of the Church, increase the value of our prayer by her intercession.[7]

Mary in the Life of the Priest

This presence was desired by Christ when on Calvary, He said to His mother, "Woman, behold your son!" Giving the beloved disciple to Mary as a gift, Jesus establishes a universal maternity through which Mary would take all Christians as her children, meaning all those called in Christ to receive salvation, in other words all men. It is a supreme gift that the Saviour gave to humanity before His death, giving His own mother to all. Each one of us receives this first fruit of the redemptive sacrifice, the mother to lead us on the way of grace who was the mother of God!

Our attention, however, is drawn to the choice of the one who was called to become Mary's son. John was a priest! Just prior to the drama on Calvary, he had received the power to celebrate the Eucharist in Christ's name: to him, as to the other apostles, the command was given: "Do this in memory of me "(*Lk* 22:19).

Having been named mother of a priest by Jesus, and being above all the mother of the High Priest Jesus, Mary became in a very special way mother of priests. She was given the task of watching over the growth of priestly life in the Church, a growth intimately linked to that of Christian life.

Jesus did not stop at entrusting to Mary this mission with regard to priests, he also addressed John, placing him in a filial relationship with Mary: "Behold your mother!" (*Jn* 19:27). He wanted the disciple to recognise Mary as his own mother and keep a deep affection for her.

The beloved disciple responded to this wish of the crucified Master by immediately taking Mary along with him. According to tradition, he experienced the first years of his apostolic ministry in the company of the one who had been given to him as mother, finding in her an incomparable helper.

"Take Mary along with you"; that is the duty and the privilege of every priest. Given the fact that he receives the power to speak and act in Christ's name, he must love Mary as Jesus loved her. In the name of this bond of filial love, he can entrust to her his priestly ministry, his projects and the difficulties he meets along the way.

Let us pray to the Virgin today that priestly formation may lead young men to "Take Mary along with them". And let us pray that the Church may be rich in priests who are increasingly more zealous in giving witness to their affection for her who has been given to them as a Mother![8]

The Man of Charity

We want to continue to reflect on who the priest is and the ideal he is meant to propose to the Church and to society. We have already seen him as a man of faith and a man of hope. Today, we see in him the man of charity. On reflection, this title is superior to the others for, according the words of Saint Paul, charity is greater than faith and hope. (1 *Co* 13:13)

When a young man feels called to the ministerial priesthood, he is, in reality, motivated by an impulse of charity, or rather by the desire to love Christ unreservedly, and to love his brothers and sisters by dedicating his entire self to them. Rightly so, because he is called to serve, as the term "minister" shows; now, in order to serve like Christ and in his name, it is necessary to love.

With ordination the young man receives a special grace of charity because the priest's life has meaning only as the fulfilment of that virtue. Christians expect the priest to be a man of God and a man of charity. Since God is love, the priest can never separate service of God from love of his brothers and sisters: committing himself to the service of God's Kingdom, the priest is committed to the path of charity. What's more, he is charged with teaching a doctrine in which the whole law is summed up in the two-fold commandment of love: love of God and love of neighbour. The priest cannot impart and spread this teaching if he himself is not an authentic witness to love.

As shepherd of Christ's flock, he cannot forget that his master ended up giving his own life out of love. In the light of such an example, the priest knows that he is no longer his own master; rather, he has the obligation of doing everything for everyone, accepting every sacrifice connected with love. This presupposes a heart which is generous and open, understanding of and well disposed to all.

Thus we can understand why preparation for the priesthood implies a serious formation in charity. The young men who are setting out on the path to the priesthood must, first of all be deeply convinced of charity's fundamental importance. The seminary in which they are trained must be an authentic place of fraternal charity, in which they can practice that virtue in the daily experience of their contact with the others. This "apprenticeship of charity" has many aspects: formation in seeking harmony despite personality differences; in being kind and in appreciating and esteeming the qualities of others; formation in immediately pardoning offences and in thoughtfully giving oneself to others.

Let us pray to the Virgin Mary, perfect model of charity in action, to help the formation of priests who are deeply motivated by Christ's charity.[9]

Priestly collaboration

When Christ instituted the priestly ministry, He did so in a communitarian form, he entrusted the pastoral office to the Twelve, calling them carry it out under the direction of Simon Peter. The priestly ministry is a collective work that all priests take part in. These who receive holy orders are destined to work together and must be formed with a spirit of collaboration. It is one of the needs of priestly formation.

Priests show the charity which inspires them in committing themselves in an organised and harmonious way to the great work of building up and developing the Christian community. We have already stressed that they must act as witnesses to Christ's charity; and this is expressed especially in the good relations which they maintain among themselves.

The spirit of mutual aid and cooperation must serve as the priest's inspiration as he carries out all his ministerial tasks. In fact, he does not undertake these tasks for personal gain or out of a spirit of ambition, but in order to respond to Christ's invitation. If he wants to accomplish Christ's work, he cannot but act in full accord with his brother priests. He will have to give them all possible help and seek to co-ordinate his actions with those of his confreres, under the particular direction which the bishop gives to pastoral work. Thus he is led to accept all the sacrifices which true co-operation requires.

The Second Vatican Council has stressed the sentiment of fraternal love which must inspire this co-operation: 'All priests who are constituted in the Order of Priesthood by the Sacrament of Orders are bound together by an intimate sacramental brotherhood" (*Presbyterorum Ordinis*, n.8). That is not just an effective but also an affective brotherhood.

In this field the formation of future priests plays an important role: formation will place the stress on the development of fraternal love among those who are preparing for the priesthood. Certainly, this fraternal love extends itself farther and takes on a universal aspect. Concretely and immediately, however, it is expressed in the living environment of the seminary and novitiate. It is there that young people learn to love one another and maintain brotherly relationships in the ambit of the community which they form.

Let us pray to the Virgin Mary that young seminarians may be formed into a priestly brotherhood which always and more vividly manifests Christ's charity.[10]

The Man of God

The first to be called to this conversion of heart are priests, they have been given a mission to encourage all men to convert, and they can only carry out this mission if they themselves are truly converted, meaning that they are turned towards God with all their heart and all their strength.

Here we are touching on a basic element in priestly formation. The priest is the man of God, the one who belongs to God and makes people think of God. When the *Letter to the Hebrews* speaks of Christ, it presents him as a "merciful and faithful high priest in the things of God" (*Heb* 2:17). This reference to God and to the things of God is contained in the definition of every priest (*cf. Heb* 5:1). The priest is responsible for humanity's relations with God: he is therefore constitutionally directed towards God, to make human offerings reach God and to lead all believing people in adoring God.

Christians hope to find in the priest not only someone who welcomes them, willingly listens to them and gives witness to his sincere love for them, but also and above all, a man who helps them to look towards God, to rise up towards him.

Therefore the priest must be trained in a deep intimacy with God. Those who prepare for the priesthood must understand that the entire worth of their priestly life will depend on the gift they are able to make of themselves to Christ and by means of Christ to the Father. Therefore they must learn to live habitually according to the dispositions suggested in Eucharistic celebration, in which the eyes of all are constantly directed towards God.

The world risks being wrapped up in itself and seeking only its own satisfactions, there must be persons capable of making the world leave that limited horizon and raise its eyes and heart towards God.

We will ask the Most Holy Virgin, who lived so intimately united to God, to help the next Synod to take those decisions which contribute towards gaining for the Church priests who are always more authentic men of God.[11]

The Man of Prayer

Prayer must truly have a place in all our lives, and at all times of the year but the forty days that precede the paschal mystery invite us to pray more intensely and more assiduously.

When Jesus spent 40 days in the desert he devoted himself to prayer. In solitude he became totally immersed in the presence of the Father; he contemplated him and dialogued with him; he entrusted his mission to him. The 40 days of prayer which preceded his preaching activity are a lesson for everyone, but especially for the priest. He is not only a man of action devoting himself to the good of those who have been entrusted to his care; he is above all a man of prayer.

Those who are preparing for it must be trained in a life of prayer. For the priest, prayer is a necessity which springs as much out of his personal life as out of his apostolic ministry. The priest needs prayer so that his life may be, as it must be, a life given in essence to Christ. It is not possible to belong to Christ with all of one's existence without maintaining a deep personal relationship with him, which is expressed through a prayer dialogue, or without directing one's eyes constantly towards him so as to live in communion with him.

The apostolic ministry demands, in its turn, constant prayer, because all of the priest's activities must be inspired by Christ and must expect fruits only as a result of his grace. The priest is called to pray for those to whom he is sent: he owes them the service of prayer, through which he can obtain for them numerous graces.

The *Letter to the Hebrews* describes Christ the priest as the one who intercedes ceaselessly for us: "He is always able to save those who approach God through him, since he lives forever to make intercession for them (*Heb* 17:25). The priest as Christ's image, must exercise a continuous mission of intercession.

Therefore, it is very important that candidates for the priesthood be trained in prayer. Above all they must have the conviction that prayer is necessary for their priestly life and their ministry. Then they must learn to pray, and to pray well, to make use of prayer time in the best way possible according to a method that suits them. Finally, they must develop a taste for prayer, the desire for it and, simultaneously, the will to pray.

We ask Mary, the Virgin at prayer, to watch over the formation of priests to prayer.[12]

The Gift of Hope

We are invited to reflect, to look into ourselves in order to have a fuller sense of our own destiny. It means thinking about the things that truly define our existence. Our gaze, and with it our thought, is often attracted by the things we see around us, so we think about fulfilling our superfluous needs and never ask ourselves what the ultimate purpose of our life is. But this question is vital, from the answer we give comes the trajectory of our earthly journey.

To discover this goal with certain clarity, we must abandon our overly superficial thoughts to make room within ourselves for divine wisdom. The Old Testament in the past recommended the search for Wisdom, which is a gift of God, but which "Is readily perceived by those who seek her" (*Ws* 6:12). Christ then, has helped us understand that he himself is Wisdom come to teach humankind.

This Wisdom must animate the priest's thoughts and direct his teaching and activities. A priest is expected not only to know the truths of the faith, but also to know how to express judgements and balanced evaluations on the basis of a personal experience of God's mystery. Whoever turns to him can count on this wisdom, which is given him from on high for the exercise of his ministry.

In particular, the priest has the task of repeating to his brothers and sisters the ultimate meaning of life, in order to direct them towards the true perspective of their existence. He must be driven by common sense and more exactly, by supernatural common sense, in order to know how to overcome with the light of grace, the too narrow viewpoints of purely human reasoning. By redirecting his eyes towards God, the priest helps those whom he meets to realise the full development of their human and Christian personality.

In the world in which we live, it is important to form candidates for the priesthood who are able to steer themselves in a balanced way through the complex experiences of life. Acquiring this maturity of judgement has an inestimable value for those who, in their ministry, must express opinions and make decisions whose consequences can be very important.

Let us pray to the Virgin Mary, Seat of Wisdom, and her spouse Joseph, that through their intercession, the Church may obtain priests who, in their wisdom, can communicate to their brothers and sisters the light they need.[13]

Collaborator With God

We are invited to rejoice, as Mary was at the time of the Annunciation. She was the first to whom the angel spoke the word "Kaire" which means "Rejoice" (Lk 1:28). Mary was able to experience all the joy offered to her because she collaborated with God fully, entirely completing the mission entrusted to her.

Let us thank Mary, for she co-operated perfectly with God, we ask her to help us to follow this way. And we implore her to aid those called to the priesthood, so that they may be ready for the challenging task of co-operating with God. The priest is in fact, called to live this co-operation in a particularly intense way.

St Paul knew this when he wrote, "We are God's fellow workers" (1 Co 3:9). He underlined the need for faithfulness that came from this point. He considered himself administrator of the divine work, an administrator who had to carry out the work according to God's intentions, being completely docile to God's plan, yet Paul worked, uniting his action with divine action. In this cooperation, he used all the qualities and resources available to him.

Christ wanted the collaborators within his church to have a pastoral responsibility, collaborators who used all their strength in the service of the kingdom he founded on earth. He did not wish to make these shepherds simple instruments of his sovereignty, he desired them to authentically collaborate with him, offering him their intelligence, their will, their efforts and all their ability and their creativity. Through the grace of ordination, the priest raised to this level of co-operation with God.

It is therefore clear that a future priest must be trained in the intimate habits that this kind of collaboration necessitates. He must become used to being docile and unreservedly faithful to divine inspiration. He must cultivate within himself, the desire to use his whole being for the service of Christ. More precisely, he must be ready for the sacrifices and privations that come with generous collaboration in the divine plan.

Mary's attitude at the moment of the Annunciation reminds us of the importance of co-operating with God, for on her answer rested the coming of the Saviour. The future of the Church in the world is also to a large extent dependent on the generosity of priestly co-operation.

May our prayer to Mary obtain numerous collaborators with God.[14]

Minister of Reconciliation

When Easter comes, Christians are encouraged to receive the Sacrament of Penance, to receive from the priest forgiveness of their sins. By the will of Christ the priest is truly the minister of reconciliation.

As you know, with the gift of the Holy Spirit the Risen Lord expressly conferred on his disciples the power to remit sins: "Receive the Holy Spirit", he said. "Whose sins you shall forgive, they are forgiven them, and whose sins you retain are retained" (*Jn* 20:22-23). This divine power has been entrusted to certain men, so that those who confess their sins *to* them may have the certainty through a visible sign that they are forgiven. This Sacrament is a wonder full invention of divine goodness; it is a source of peace and joy.

Conscious of God's loving plan, St Paul considered himself responsible for the "ministry of reconciliation" and urged the Christians of Corinth: "Be reconciled to God". Indeed, he knew how to be Christ's ambassador, or more particularly, the ambassador of God's desire to forgive, which was fully revealed in the sacrifice of the Cross, when God reconciled us to himself through Christ (*cf. 2 Co* 5:18-20).

The priest has inherited from the apostles the noble task of reconciling people with God in the name of Christ. Like St Paul, he also, as Christ's ambassador, exhorts Christians to be reconciled to God through the sacrament whose purpose is to grant pardon. I am confident that, Christians in the whole Church will use this sacrament to advantage, in order to receive, along with forgiveness, a new impulse towards holiness.

In its reflections on priestly formation the Synod will not fail to take into consideration the preparation of future ministers for this Sacrament which is so important in the life of the Church. In this case preparing oneself means first of all developing a sense of sin in oneself, the awareness of the offence we give God by disobeying his law. In today's world the sense of sin seems frequently to be lost. The future priest must deepen in himself the awareness of the serious evil which sin involves.

Furthermore, the candidate to the priesthood will seek to assimilate more and more the sentiments of Christ, who showed great kindness to those who committed evil, so much so that he was called a friend of sinners (cf. *Mt* 11:19). The candidate should learn to cultivate a deep "sympathy" for those who err, with the constant desire to obtain their salvation.

Today we want to pray to the Virgin most pure and merciful, that through priestly formation the Synod may foster the exercise of the ministry of reconciliation.[15]

Missionary Eagerness

At Pentecost we see the apostles witnessing to the marvels of God before people from every corner of the earth. From the moment of its birth, the Church has been missionary. The first priests, the apostles were driven by the Spirit to travel to every part of the world. How can we not see in this a clear indication as to the missionary side of all priestly ministry?

It often happens that the term missionary is used to refer only to those who devote themselves to evangelisation in distant lands. Although we pay the greatest tribute to this generous form of self-giving which shows how far a love totally dedicated to Christ can go, we must reaffirm that the entire Christian community is missionary by virtue of the universal and undivided divine plan of salvation. Missionary zeal, therefore, must be felt and shared by all Christians, and by all priests in particular.

In the Church priesthood is essentially missionary, and every priest must be well aware of this.

Indeed, there are many occasions for the priest to exercise his ministry in a missionary perspective and avoid being unduly wrapped up only in his community.

Being informed and telling the faithful about the Church's situation in mission lands, inviting them to pray for the missions and to make their own concrete contribution for its needs, he participates in the Church's missionary effort and shares in the task of service for the spread of God's Kingdom in the world.

Priestly formation, therefore, must be a training in the missionary spirit. The seminary staff will interest the young men in the Church's missionary apostolate so that the candidates for the priesthood do not see only the world of the diocese to which they belong, but the wider horizons of the universal Church. The coming Synod will study the means to use in this field to achieve a priestly training that is open to all the world's needs.

We shall now pray to Mary Most Holy, who shares the tumultuous Pentecost experience with the primitive community and bears witness to its initial opening up to the world - let us pray that she will help to prepare for the Church priests who are moved by an ardent missionary spirit. To her, Queen of the Missions, we commend this holy cause of the Church of God.[16]

Guided by the Holy Spirit

The priestly ministry is exercised in the name of Christ but is the work of the Holy Spirit, for it is through the Spirit that the Saviour shows his holiness and gives his life to humanity. At the moment of his ordination, it is the Holy Spirit that makes the priest capable of completing his mission.

Priestly formation is a training for the ministry of the Spirit (*cf. 2 Co* 3:6, 8). The candidate to the priesthood must become accustomed to living and acting in intimate union with the Holy Spirit. Formation has the purpose of preparing for ordination men who "are filled with the Spirit and Wisdom", according to St Peter's request for the first ordination of ministers in the Church's service (*Ac* 6:3).

The priest needs the Holy Spirit's impulse and light in exercising the various functions proper to him. In proclaiming the word, he must implore the Spirit's light that he may better understand the meaning of the doctrine which he must teach and express it faithfully in a way that is adapted to his listeners. When the priest celebrates the Eucharist, in the *epiclesis* he invokes the Holy Spirit for the transformation of bread and wine into the Body and Blood of Christ and for the efficacy of the banquet of communion. When he administers the sacraments, he acts under the influence of the Holy Spirit, the author of all holiness. In his function as pastor by which he leads the community, he cannot fulfil his task if he does not abandon himself to the Holy Spirit's guidance.

Therefore, the enlightened priest will not rely on his own talents, but on the hidden strength of the Holy Spirit who acts in him to spread Christ's life in human hearts. Personal plans, programmes and efforts produce results only with the invisible, often unforeseeable and always sovereign influence of the Holy Spirit, accustomed to relying on the Holy Spirit in exercising his mission, the priest will also be led to recognise and respect the Spirit's action in his co-workers and in all members of the Christian community. Let us pray to Mary, who opened her heart widely to the action of the Holy Spirit that she may obtain for the Church priests who are true ministers of the Spirit.[17]

Witness to the Risen One

The duty to bear witness is one laid on all Christians but with particular earnestness it is laid on priests.

The priest is called to be a witness to the Risen Christ invisibly but truly present in his Church which is committed to bringing the Gospel proclamation to all nations. In order to bear such witness effectively, the priest must believe without hesitation that Christ overcame death and has become the centre of a new humanity.

Dearly beloved, sometimes Christianity is presented as a religion of pure resignation, or passive acceptance, which diminishes the human person, or as one that is exclusively centred on suffering and darkens the horizons of human thought and life. On the contrary, the religion of the Risen Christ is a proclamation of life, with the new life of Christ it develops all the energies of the person and bears witness that suffering is a passage to a greater joy.

It is the Resurrection event which gives the Christian religion its true aspect. Certainly, it does not take away the need for the Christian to experience Christ's Cross and to suffer the passing triumph of the forces of evil.

The priest must also live this truth in the exercise of his ministry by strengthening his confidence in the Saviour's victory over the forces of evil. Thus he will have an optimistic outlook on the world, relying on the secret action of redeeming grace and overcoming all disappointments and unexpected problems with the strength of his hope.

Each day the priest must be open to the joy which the Risen Christ made definitive in human destiny; in this joy he must overcome all sorrows and trials. This witness of joy is the only one in harmony with the good news, which can not be proclaimed in any way other than as a message of happiness.

Let us now pray to the Virgin Mary that candidates to the priesthood, may become authentic witnesses to the Risen Christ, the giver of life.[18]

Minister of the Eucharist

When, during the Angelus we say, "The Word was made flesh and dwelt amongst us", we remember the central mystery of the incarnation, which in a particular and sacramental way, continues through the Eucharist. In every Eucharistic celebration, the Word, made flesh comes to dwell in our midst.

The fundamental importance of the Eucharist in the life of the Church makes us understand the irreplaceable role of the priestly ministry. Without priests there can be no Eucharistic offering. For this reason the Second Vatican Council affirms that when celebrating the Eucharistic ministry priest exercise their principle function. In their capacity as ministers of things sacred, they are above all ministers of the sacrifice of the mass (cf. "*Presb. Ordinis*", 13) The Eucharist constitutes the apex of the Church's sacramental life. It is also the sacrament that exercises the greatest influence over the Christian's daily life. Those who enter the priestly ministry must be trained in a special way for Eucharistic ministry. Candidates for ordination must be formed in an intense faith in the Eucharist. At the very first announcement of this Sacrament, Jesus asked his apostles - or those who would be the first to exercise the priestly ministry - for an act of faith in the Eucharist. It was Peter who, in the name of the Twelve, made the first profession of faith. This shows that the priest, who is responsible for the Eucharistic celebration in the Church, must be motivated by a strong faith in the sacramental offering of Christ, in the gift he makes of his body and blood through Communion, and in his permanent presence in the Eucharist which Christians are invited to adore.

It is therefore recommended that seminarians attend the Eucharistic celebration every day, so that, with time, this daily celebration will become a rule of their priestly life.

In addition they will be trained to regard the Eucharistic celebration as the culminating moment of their day, at which they will become accustomed to participate actively, never contenting themselves with simply passive attendance.

Lastly, the candidates to the priesthood will be trained thoroughly in the inner dispositions which the Eucharist promotes: gratitude for benefits received from above, since Eucharist means thanksgiving; an attitude of self-sacrifice, which will prompt them to unite their own personal offering to the Eucharistic offering of Christ; charity nourished by the Sacrament which is a sign of unity and of sharing; and the desire to contemplate and adore Christ truly visible under the form of the Eucharistic presence.

We pray that the Virgin Mary may intercede with the Son, to obtain many faithful Eucharistic ministers.[19]

Evangelical Poverty

"He has filled the starving with good things and sent the rich away empty." (*Lk* 1:53)

With these words from the "Magnificat" the Blessed Virgin reminds all of us of God's preferential love for the poor. In his goodness God the Father is pleased to fill with graces persons who, deprived of material riches, do not seek their happiness in this world's goods.

Those called to priestly ministry are invited in a special way to keep their distance from money and worldly goods. Certainly as the Conciliar Decree "*Presbyterorum Ordinis*" observed, priests need resources to lead their personal lives and to fulfil their mission: "Let priests be thankful," recommends the document, "for everything that the Heavenly Father has given them for a proper standard of living. However, they ought to judge everything they meet in the light of faith, so that they will be guided towards the right use of things in accordance with God's will and will reject anything that is prejudicial to their own mission" (*n.* 17).

Seminarians must be prepared for their ministry with a mentality of pure dedication and of profound selflessness.

The Second Vatican Council recalls that they "are invited to embrace voluntary poverty. By it they become more clearly conformed to Christ and more ready to devote themselves to their sacred ministry. For Christ, being rich, became poor for our sakes, that through his poverty we might be rich. The Apostles by their example gave testimony that the free gift of God was to be given freely. They knew both how to abound and to suffer need" (*ibid.*).

Training given in the seminary will place young men within reach of that poverty which Christ practiced and wished for those to whom he entrusted the main pastoral duty in his Church. That will prepare them to be witnesses to the spiritual kingdom, through renouncing the search for material wealth. It will give them a taste of simplicity of lifestyle, sheltering them from every temptation to luxury or excessive comfort.

This is an important witness in a world which is often dominated by the struggles of self-interest and conflicts of a monetary nature. The priest has the mission of showing that human destiny does not lie in accumulating earthly goods, because there are other values, much higher ones, which merit being pursued with perseverance - those, that is, which ennoble the person and lead him or her to enter in to a communion of life with God.

Priestly formation will also tend to foster in seminarians the desire to help the poor and to proclaim the Good News to them, after the example and teachings of Christ. It will encourage them to be sympathetically disposed towards them and to give the neediest a preferential love.

Let us pray to the Virgin Mary that she may show the way to proceed towards an effective training of priests in evangelical poverty.[20]

The Minister of Obedience

The Angelus makes us repeat the words the Virgin Mary used to express her complete acceptance of the divine plan for her life. Putting herself completely in God's hands, she foreshadowed the One who would be sent to earth by the Father, the One who always submitted to his will.

The Letter to the Hebrews (*Heb* 5:8) points out the value of this obedience of the Son of God, when He entered this world and offered His sacrifice. In His suffering, Christ, the priest, experienced obedience, as the Son, which was the source of the graces He gained for the Salvation of humanity.

The importance of obedience in the priestly life should be understood in this light. "Of all the virtues most necessary for the ministry of the priest," says the Second Vatican Council, "one that should not be overlooked is the spirit to search, not for the satisfaction of their own desires, but the fulfilment of the will of the One who sent them." (*Presbyterorum Ordinis*, 15) Those who prepare for the priesthood must therefore be formed to this fundamental acquiescence to the will of the Father. The Council particularly stressed the ecclesial aspect of the obedience of priests. "The priestly ministry, since it is the ministry of the Church itself, can only function in the hierarchical union of the whole body. Pastoral charity, therefore, urges priests, as they operate in the framework of this union, to dedicate their own will by obedience to the service of God and their fellow men. In a great spirit of faith, let them receive and execute whatever orders the Holy Father, their own bishop, or other superiors give or recommend.

With a willing heart let them spend and even exhaust themselves in whatever task they are given, even though it be menial and unrecognised. (*Presbyterorum Ordinis*, 15)

The council adds that through this obedience, priests can be sure of being united, not only with the visible head of the Church, but also with their brothers in the ministry. Note that this does not curtail initiative or the spirit to search for new ways of completing their pastoral work, on condition that this inventiveness is exercised while submitting to authority.

Vatican II brought to light and clearly stated the reciprocal duties of bishops and priests in this delicate matter. It recommended to the former that, motivated by their communion in the same priestly ministry they "Should regard priests as their brothers and friends and be concerned as far as they are able for their material and especially for their spiritual well-being," and reminded priests that "never losing sight of the fullness of the priesthood which the bishops enjoy, must respect in them the authority of Christ, the Supreme Shepherd. They must therefore stand by their bishops in sincere charity and obedience." (*Presbyterorum Ordinis*, 15)

Seminarians must receive a formation in the context of this wide-ranging theological and ascetic vision that means they will become more used to and disposed to obeying authority. It is an obedience motivated by faith, that recognises in the decisions of those in authority the divine will, an obedience that cannot take place without certain sacrifices, but that all make the priestly ministry fruitful. Above all, it associates the priest with the obedience that characterised the sacrifice of the cross and the fruits of that sacrifice.

We pray, most holy Mary, model of docility to divine will, from the "fiat" of the Annunciation to the painful maternity on Calvary, that you may help all those preparing for the priesthood to enter, knowingly and joyously into the ministry of obedience.[21]

Forming the Formators

The central event of history, the incarnation of the Son of God, which we remember reciting the Angelus, emphasises the eminent qualities of the most holy Virgin Mary. She was filled with grace because she would co-operate in a unique way, with the life, growth and mission of Jesus.

This example is without compare: yet it helps us to understand as well the importance of the quality of educators in priestly formation. Those who have the mission of preparing young men for priestly life and ministry are called to a great responsibility.

"Seminary superiors and professors should therefore be chosen from among the best," says Vatican II, "and should receive a careful preparation in sound doctrine, suitable pastoral experience and special training in spirituality and teaching methods" (*Optatam Totius*, n .5).

It is true that only divine grace can render a person fit to accomplish well the task of educator in a seminary or, in regard to religious, in a house of formation. This grace will not be lacking because Christ who during his earthly life devoted himself so intensely and, I would say, exclusively to the preparation of the apostles, now continues to keep watch over the formation of priests and obtains all the graces necessary for that task.

On their part, formators must be open to these graces and rely on them. They must therefore have an intense spiritual life, bear witness to a sincere faith which inspires their entire behaviour. This witness must be evident in their whole way of thinking and acting. "Superiors and professors," the Council declaration continues, "should be keenly aware of the extent to which their mental outlook and conduct affect the formation of their students" (*ibid.*).

If they live out their priesthood fully, they can communicate the meaning of the beauty of a life entirely consecrated to Christ, and confirm young men entrusted to their care in the grace of the vocation. They will help them overcome their problems on the path towards priestly ordination, and will encourage them to make the needed effort to prepare themselves for it, by accepting the joys and the sacrifices which priestly life carries with it.

And it is especially to be hoped that superiors and educators form a real "communion" of prayer, study and action with the seminarians, intended to develop the vocations of the young men; to that end, their personal commitment to intellectual and spiritual formation and their fraternal relationships with the seminarians are very important. In particular, they will seek to foster a climate of generosity and joy, as well as the active desire to devote themselves fully one day to the apostolic and pastoral mission.

Let us ask Most Holy Mary to obtain through her maternal intercession, numerous educators gifted with excellent qualities for the formation of candidates to the priesthood.[22]

Mary: Teacher of Young Men
Called to the Priesthood

We have an opportunity to return to her specific role in the formation of priests. I have already spoken on another occasion of the importance of Mary in the life of the priest. Today I want to look more closely at her role as the teacher of priests.

That specific role emerges from the "educational" mission given to Mary as Jesus was growing up. By calling Mary "Mother of God," Christians have recognised the greatness of the motherhood of her who was called to bear a child who was God. But the noble nature of this motherly formation did not stop at the act of giving life to the child; it was revealed in his upbringing. Mary had received all the graces necessary to train Jesus, to prepare Him for His priestly mission. In this way she was the perfect educator of the one and eternal Priest.

More especially, the Holy Spirit inspired in her a readiness to serve, as expressed in the words of the Angelus: "Behold the handmaid of the Lord "(*Lk* 1:38). This service to the Lord quickly extended to service of others, as is seen by the journey which she made to be near Elizabeth.

Mary contributed to the development of Jesus' spirit of service, which was constantly evident in the way in which she forgot herself, to devote herself entirely to others. In every circumstance of life in Nazareth, Jesus was able to admire the readiness and the tireless spirit of service of his mother.

In his public life, then, this spirit of service is the element that defined Jesus' very mission: "The Son of Man came not to be served but to serve and to give his life as a ransom for many" (*Mk* 10:45; *Mt* 20:28). Thereby he wanted to give a lesson to his disciples who sought to satisfy their own personal ambition in some fashion.

The priesthood to which they were destined cannot be lived out therefore, "By being served, but through service"; the term "ministry" means precisely "service". The ministerial priesthood consists in serving others.

Thus the influence which Mary can have on priestly formation in training in a spirit of service is clear. She who was the educator of the one Priest remains the educator *par excellence* of young men called to the priesthood. So that she might be permitted to carry out that function, she must be recognised in devotions and prayer as the one who helps seminarians to enter into that basic attitude of service which allows them to carry out priestly ministry.

We pray that the place which belongs to Mary in the formation of future priests, ministers, that is, servants of God's people may become ever clearer.[23]

Love for the Sick

Among the tasks of the priestly ministry is visiting the sick, which gives them moral and spiritual strength to bear with the trial of their sickness and overcome it.

In the Gospel we constantly note the special attention Jesus gave the sick. It is a mark of his activity: St Matthew says that "Jesus went around to all the towns and villages, teaching in their synagogues, proclaiming the Gospel of the Kingdom, and curing every disease and illness" (*Mt* 9:35); St Luke says that "great crowds assembled to listen to him and to be cured of their ailments" (*Lk* 5, 16).

With a compassion directed to the sick and the infirm, Jesus revealed the Love of God who stoops down with infinite mercy in the face of all human misery. At the same time he reveals effective compassion: he not only showed sympathy, but obtained healing. By working many miracles for the sick, he showed that God places his almighty power at the service of humanity.

The priest is called to follow the example of Christ and offer the Saviour's full concern to the sick. Unlike Christ, he does not have the power to heal the sick and the infirm, but he can give them moral and spiritual consolation which will support them in their trials and will serve to facilitate and accelerate their healing. By prayer too, the priest asks for and obtains an improvement in the condition of the sick who are entrusted to his care.

His pastoral ministry leads him to practise love towards the most wretched, as the Gospel highly urges. Each time the priest visits a sick person, he is invited to see in them the mysterious presence of Christ: "I was sick and you visited Me" (*Mt* 25:36). In the sufferings of the sick he respectfully and lovingly recognises the mystery of Christ crucified which continues in human lives.

Within the context of the work of salvation, the priest is called to visit the sick. Jesus multiplied miraculous healings as a sign of the healing he wanted to gain for all humanity. His physical healings did not have only one aim, he wanted to save people from evil. Therefore we see him forgiving the paralytic's sins before healing him and then carrying out the miracle to show that the pardon actually occurred.

The priest will always have the goal of his mission before his eyes: the full salvation of the person which takes place above all on the spiritual level. He knows that sickness is a time of testing but also of grace, and he will encourage the sick to profit from these graces to draw closer to Christ; to discover His mysterious presence; to accept the Father's will and to offer him their suffering with a more selfless spirit.

Let us ask the Virgin Mary, who had such a compassionate heart, to guide priests with her motherly care during their visits, and to encourage them continually in this very important ministry.[24]

Celibacy: A Greater Love

Our Saviour was born of a Virgin. Mary's virginity, which the mystery of the incarnation necessitated, was a prelude to the virgin life of Christ. It was part of God's plan that a virgin should prepare Jesus for his priestly ministry, which required him to remain celibate.

Here we find the primary origin of the choice of life to which, according to the Latin Church's discipline, priests are called. According to the principle expressed by the Council in the Decree *Optatam Totius*: "Students who follow the venerable tradition of priestly celibacy as laid down by the holy and permanent regulations of their own rite should be very carefully trained for this state. In it they renounce marriage for the sake of the kingdom of heaven (cf. *Mt* 19:12) and hold fast to their Lord with that undivided love which is profoundly in harmony with the New Covenant; they bear witness to the resurrection in a future life (cf. *Lk* 20:36) and obtain the most useful assistance towards the constant exercise of that perfect charity by which they can become all things to all men in their priestly ministry" (*n.* 10).

In the Gospel, Christ did not hesitate to ask those whom he chose as apostles to leave everything to follow him. Leaving everything also means renouncing having a family of one's own. More than anyone else, Jesus knew that such a renunciation demands much generosity because it requires the total gift of self. The absolute master of human life, he invited the apostles to commit themselves in such a gift, because he saw its fruitfulness.

It is true that consecrated celibacy requires a special grace because it is an ideal which is beyond the strength of human nature and sacrifices some of its inclinations. The Lord, however, who guided his Church in the choice of this path, will not fail to give this grace to those whom he calls to the priesthood. Through such a gift from on high, they will be able to assume the commitment and remain faithful to it for their entire life.

We must, however, prepare the young men who enter the seminary to understand more clearly the motives for and demands of this choice, accepting in prayer the grace which is given them. They will be more aware of the dangers to which they could be exposed and the humble prudence which they must have in their behaviour. Most of all, they should be strengthened in the conviction that celibacy is essentially a greater love for Christ and one's neighbour, and that it is destined to support the holiness and fidelity of Christian couples.

Let us ask the intercession of the Virgin of virgins, that she may ensure that the young men who are preparing for priesthood receive an adequate training in regard to the demands of this greater love.[25]

The Man of Sacrifice

We repeat our profession of faith in the Word that "Was made flesh and dwelt amongst us." He came to redeem us, to suffer and die for us. With the incarnation, begins the stripping which will reach its zenith when Christ humbles himself, "Being obedient until death, death on a cross." (Ph 2:8)

Before the crucifix, each one of us can say with the Apostle Paul: "I live by faith in the Son of God who has loved me and given himself up for me" (*Ga* 2:20). The Incarnation, Passion and Death of Christ lead us into the contemplation of an unfathomable mystery of love. It is this mystery which allows us to understand fully the meaning of our trials, they unite us to the cross of Christ and his redemptive work. St Paul explained the suffering of his own life, saying: "I have been crucified with Christ" (*Ga* 2:19). He suffered greatly in the apostolic ministry, but he understood the deeper meaning of these sufferings.

In this way an essential aspect of priestly life is clarified: the priest is a man of sacrifice. By virtue of the Sacrament of Orders he has the mission of offering Christ's sacrifice, making Him mystically present in the reality of His Body and Blood. As a consequence, by his priestly existence itself he is united to Christ's redemptive sacrifice. Priestly ordination commits him to a life of sacrifice.

Jesus asked a question of the apostles who were tempted to see their involvement in building the kingdom as only an honour, "Can you drink the cup that I drink?" (*Mk* 10:38). He then went on to explain the reason for this essential question, "The Son of Man did not come to be served but to serve and to give his life as a ransom for many" (*Mk* 10:45). If the Master followed the way of the cross, how could those whom he called to share in his mission ever think of taking a different path?

The priest knows that he is called to sacrifice in a special way. Nonetheless, he will find the strength to bear his trials, which are often difficult ones, in a spirit of generosity, if he is able to see them in the light of Christ's passion. Did St Paul not say, "Now I rejoice in my sufferings for your sake, and in my flesh I am filling up what is lacking in the afflictions of Christ on behalf of his Body, which is the Church" (*Col* 1:24)?

Those who are preparing for the priesthood must develop a spirit of generosity which will make them capable of accepting the necessary renunciation for love of Christ, recognising its apostolic fruitfulness.

The Virgin Mary, standing at the foot of the Cross, helps us understand that one cannot be united to Christ without sharing in his sacrifice. Let us pray to her that she may sustain priests in their trials and that, through appropriate training, she may lead them to accept courageously the sacrifices demanded by their ministry.[26]

The Whole Church Relies on the Holy Spirit

The Holy Spirit understands what is necessary in order to form priests, infinitely better than any of us. The Holy Spirit knows what the priestly ministry consists of and how it should truly be lived.

Was it not the Holy Spirit who at the moment of the Incarnation brought about in a decisive way the human nature of the first priest? Was it not to him that Jesus attributed a special influence upon his entire earthly ministry, when in the Nazareth synagogue he applied Isaiah's prophetic utterance to himself, "The Spirit of the Lord is upon me" (*Lk* 4:18). This decisive role of the Spirit in the formation of the High Priest shows us that it is really to the Spirit that we must entrust our efforts towards the formation of those who today must reproduce in their own lives the model given by Christ by imitating him in his life and mission.

Therefore, the whole Church counts on the Holy Spirit. The Holy Spirit will not be absent from, nor fail to act. Trusting in the Spirit's help, may Mary Most Holy help everyone to open themselves up completely to his action.[27]

Servant of the Lord

The people of God desire priests who are prepared to live holy lives, who are knowledgeable in faith and zealous in their pastoral work, priests ready for the new evangelisation our times necessitate.

We invoke the Virgin, Mother of Christ and Mother of all priests, in the sure knowledge that she who is "full of grace", is the true model for each priest consecrated to the service of the Kingdom. Mary was, in fact, eternally present in God's plan for the salvation of the world. Through faith she participated in it throughout her whole earthly journey, so that today she is the model for all those who are called to follow Jesus, master and shepherd of souls, ever more closely.

May the intercession of Mary help candidates to the priestly ministry to be attentive to the Word of God, unreservedly accepting his demands and preparing themselves to share in Christ's sentiments, so that they may become effective messengers of His mystery. It is necessary for priests to be, like Mary, humble servants of the Lord, in order for them to become, like her, effective instruments of the "great things" that God in tends for the world.

May the Blessed Virgin accompany all those who have been called on their formation journey. May she be for them a comfort and support in their trials, a model in consecrating all their affection and interests to the cause of the salvation of people. As a watchful Mother, may she be present to enlighten and strengthen the resolutions of the young men whom the Lord has called to follow him.[28]

Prayers

Prayer For the Year of the Priest

Lord Jesus,

In Saint John Mary Vianney you have gifted to the Church a living image of your pastoral charity.

May we live this Year of the Priest in his company and led by his example.

Grant that we may learn from the from him how to rest contentedly before the Holy Eucharist, knowing that only your Word enlightens us each day, knowing how tender is the love with which you welcome repentant sinners and how consoling is the confident abandonment to the care of your Holy and Immaculate Mother.

Grant O Lord Jesus, that by the intercession of the saintly Curé of Ars, Christian families may become "little Churches", in which all the vocations and charisms given by the Holy Spirit may be welcomed and valued. Allow us Lord Jesus, to repeat with the same ardour, the words the holy Curé used when he turned to you.

I love You, O my God and my sole desire is to love You until the last breath of my life.

I love You, O infinitely lovable God and I prefer to die loving You than live one instant without loving You.

I love You, O my God, and the only grace I ask of You is that of loving You eternally. O my God, if my tongue cannot say in every moment that I love You, I want my heart to say it in every beat.

I love You O my divine Saviour, because you were crucified for me, and you keep me here, crucified with you. My God, give me the grace to die loving you and knowing that I love you. Amen[29]

To Mary, Queen of Apostles

O, Mary, Queen of apostles,
teach those who are called this duty
to have their hearts shaped in the school of the divine master,
your Son Jesus.
Give to those who have been called to the priesthood
The longing for what is truly great,
The desire for evangelic perfection,
The will to save souls,
the courage and generosity to follow Jesus wherever He goes.
Support those future workers of the harvest, in all the steps in their journey to the altar,
In all their choices connected with true ecclesial service,
in all the sacrifices necessary in serving Christ with undivided heart.
May new priests be able to understand the "secrets" of God,
may they respond speedily,
to anyone's petition,

may they be open to their problems,
especially those of the poorest and most humble,
imitating the generous dedication of your son Jesus.
May they, through prayer, through the Eucharist, through
meditating on the revealed Word, find the strength to
become everyday, evermore holy.
Amen.[30]

To Mary, Mother of Priests

O Mary,
Mother of Jesus Christ and Mother of priests, accept this
title which we bestow on you
to celebrate your motherhood and to contemplate with
you the priesthood of, your Son and of your sons,

O holy Mother of God. O Mother of Christ, to the
Messiah - priest you gave a body of flesh through the
anointing of the Holy Spirit for the salvation of the poor
and the contrite of heart; guard priests in your heart and
in the Church, O Mother of the Saviour.

O Mother of Faith, you accompanied to the Temple the Son
of Man, the fulfillment of the promises given to the fathers;
give to the Father for his glory the priests of your Son,
O Ark of the Covenant.
O Mother of the Church, in the midst of the disciples in
the upper room,
you prayed to the Spirit for the new people and their

shepherds; obtain for the Order of Presbyters a full measure of gifts, O Queen of the Apostles.

O Mother of Jesus Christ, you were with him at the beginning of his life and mission, you sought the Master among the crowd, you stood beside him when he was lifted up from the earth consumed as the one eternal sacrifice, and you had John, your son, near at hand; accept from the beginning those who have been called,
protect their growth, in their life-ministry accompany your sons, O Mother of Priests.
Amen.[31]

Endnotes

[1] 3rd December 1989.

[2] 10th December 1989.

[3] 17th December 1989.

[4] 24th December 1989.

[5] 31st December 1989.

[6] 14th January 1990.

[7] 4th February 1990.

[8] 11th February 1990.

[9] 18th February 1990.

[10] 25th February 1990.

[11] 4th March 1990.

[12] 11th March 1990.

[13] 18th March 1990.

[14] 25th March 1990.

[15] 1st April 1990.

[16] 3rd June 1990.

[17] 10th June 1990.

[18] 24th June 1990.

[19] 1st July 1990.

[20] 8th July 1990.

[21] 12th July 1990.

[22] 29th July 1990.

[23] 5th August 1990.

[24] 12th August 1990.

[25] 19th August 1990.

[26] 16th September 1990.

[27] 30th September 1990.

[28] 28th October 1990.

[29] Pope Benedict XVI.

[30] John Paul II, 2nd July 1990.

[31] *Pastores dabo vobis*, 25th March 1992.